Inside the Pearl

ESSENTIAL POETS SERIES 290

Guernica Editions Inc. acknowledges the support of
the Canada Council for the Arts and the Ontario Arts Council.
The Ontario Arts Council is an agency of the Government of Ontario.
We acknowledge the financial support of the Government of Canada

Jude Neale

Inside the Pearl

Photos by Paul Hooson

GUERNICA
EDITIONS

TORONTO • CHICAGO • BUFFALO • LANCASTER (U.K.)
2021

Michael Mirolla, editor
Cover and interior design: Rafael Chimicatti
Cover Image: Paul Hooson
Interior Photos: Paul Hooson

Guernica Editions Inc.
287 Templemead Dr., Hamilton, Ontario, Canada L8W 2W4
2250 Military Road, Tonawanda, N.Y. 14150-6000 U.S.A.
www.guernicaeditions.com

Distributors:
Independent Publishers Group (IPG)
600 North Pulaski Road, Chicago IL 60624
University of Toronto Press Distribution (UTP)
5201 Dufferin Street, Toronto (ON), Canada M3H 5T8
Gazelle Book Services
White Cross Mills, High Town, Lancaster LA1 4XS U.K.

First edition.
Printed in Canada.

Legal Deposit – Third Quarter
Library of Congress Catalog Card Number: 2021932977
Library and Archives Canada Cataloguing in Publication
Title: Inside the pearl / Jude Neale.
Names: Neale, Jude, author.
Series: Essential poets ; 290.
Description: First edition. | Series statement: Essential poets series ; 290 | Poems.
Identifiers: Canadiana 20210140593 | ISBN 9781771836746 (softcover)
Classification: LCC PS8627.E22 I57 2021 | DDC C811/.6—dc23

And I remember how careful my parents were
Not to bruise us with bitterness ...
—Joy Kogawa

*Dedicated to those who face injustice
with courage and integrity*

Foreword

Welcome to this beautiful collection of short poems and images, composed during a residency at Historic Joy Kogawa House, the childhood home of author Joy Kogawa. Jude Neale is one of more than forty writers who have used this space to create new work, sometimes successfully published, other times rewritten over years before it finds its way to readers. As host to these resident writers, I am always interested to read the work in progress, to support writers along their way, and to learn more about how the space inspires their work. In return, each resident responds to the history of Joy Kogawa House in new ways.

The poems Jude shares here add to the story of the house and are a particular gift in support of our author residencies. These poems reveal intense personal emotion about the house and the past it represents. In clear and precise words, Jude confronts and contains the lingering legacies of this country's national history: the internment of Japanese Canadians that author Joy Kogawa experienced as a child and then shared in her novels, poems, a memoir—and now an immersive app titled *East of the Rockies* with the National Film Board of Canada—all of which document her memory of this place. Joy Kogawa's writing describes this tiny Marpole house as a way of coming to know the trauma of displacement from homes and properties that she and her family and 22,000 other Japanese Canadians experienced during the Second World War. Although this place is materially real and provides a spatial fix to Joy's writing and the time before internment, it is a space that writers continue to make and remake in the present. For as Karen Till says, "Places are not only continuously interpreted but, when people inhabit places of memory, they often uncover and make visible a material embodiment of their own past. They imprint upon and interact with items and objects to create a new and artistic response to the place and its past."

As a national place of memory, Historic Joy Kogawa House remembers the past along with unnamed, yet powerfully felt, absences, displacements, removals, loss.

The heritage and cultural site serves as an eyewitness to history and traces stories from another time. We hope that by visiting this place and others like it we can experience, and perhaps work through, contradictory emotions associated with past wrongs, including fear, anger, guilt, shame, sadness, longing, and unease. By representing place in these ways, we create a social space defined by contemporary needs and desires; we emplace Joy Kogawa's social dream for inclusion with her own and our resident writers' hopes for the future.

Thank you for purchasing this book in support of Historic Joy Kogawa House and thank you to Jude Neale and Paul Hooson for gifting us these poems and images to add to the story of Joy Kogawa's longed-for home. "We never lived in such a beautiful house again."

Ann-Marie Metten
Executive Director of Historic Joy Kogawa House

Preface

I first became aware of Joy Kogawa when I read *Obasan*. This was her account of internment in Canada because she is a Canadian of Japanese heritage, in and beyond the Second World War.

The novel opened my eyes to injustice, betrayal, and loss. Impossible truths to a young, white, privileged woman.

Joy moved me to do better. To think critically and try in my own way to act out of love.

This book, *Inside the Pearl*, was created inside the space Joy loved, and the poems rose out of my propensity for intense scrutiny and rampant curiosity. I took hundreds of pictures and wrote close to sixty haiku inspired imagistic poems during my time there. I decided to document it, inside and out. I was an archaeologist of the half remembered. I pulled things out of drawers, looked in corners, even opened suitcases.

Opened suitcases! To my wonder and disbelief, I had unearthed a representation of the few things the family had taken to the Slocan. A precious blanket. Beloved doll dresses. Well-worn books. A toy car. I felt like I was gifted with insight into the extraordinary times that Joy Kogawa lived. That picture became the backbone of this book which is why I chose it for the cover. It spoke of displacement and loss and endings.

I hope that both my written images and Paul Hooson's photographs in this volume shine a light on the many small things that make a home. Notes scrawled, white curtains blowing in the breeze, or the comfort of a feather bed.

Inside the Pearl speaks of simple things and presents like snapshots, another time on the page.

My gratitude to Joy Kogawa for creating a bridge to truth for all peoples through her exceptional writing and quiet, gentle strength.

Jude Neale

About the Photographs

The photographs you see in this book come from a place of quiet but acute observation of Joy Kogawa's early life, as seen through the lens of her former house and the objects that inhabit its rooms, walls, drawers, and wainscoted corners.

My role in this residency was initially that of a cultural archaeologist, bringing Jude artifacts, information, and taking photographs to stimulate her imagination and accompany the poems. I poked into every nook and cranny of the dwelling, placing no bounds on my curiosity.

The poetry that emerged was a stunning collection, capturing an intensely precious but traumatic time in Joy's life, and that of the greater Japanese Canadian community. We realized that the photos had a powerful impact when presented, together. The visual context augmented the text in an almost tactile way, forming a photo-essay to accompany the poems. As such, they became an integral part of the finished manuscript.

These images are amateur snapshots, but I think their spontaneity and raw simplicity serve the style and underlying aesthetic of the book This is what we saw with our own eyes, during our stay. Some are historic in nature, others almost still-life studies. Many contain subtle references reflecting the nuanced nature of Jude Neale's work, but all will hopefully serve to enrich the reader's experience of this place, that time, and the amazing person who is Joy Kogawa.

Paul Hooson

Acknowledgements

Before I was writer-in-residence at Historic Joy Kogawa House I had mapped out a plan for my stay there. I would write sixty haiku-inspired imagistic poems accompanied by sixty photographs. An archival collection about the many ordinary objects I saw there.

The executive director of Historic Joy Kogawa House, Ann-Marie Metten, is the repository of so much Historic Joy Kogawa House knowledge. She met my idea at once with enthusiasm. She provided support and wisdom throughout this project for which I am so grateful.

The great writer and editor, Jacqueline Pearce, threw me a lifeline—links to national and international haiku sites. It was from these places I gradually pieced together what a haiku was, so that my imagistic writing could have a haiku flavour. I sent my tenth iteration off to Jacquie, and she in one email acted as editor, coach, mentor, and colleague. She was an invaluable resource in my quest to understand further this complex and beautiful art form.

I would also like to give special mention to my partner, Paul Hooson. This project was truly a labour of love for us both.

We respectfully acknowledge that Historic Joy Kogawa House is situated on the traditional, ancestral, and unceded lands of the Squamish, Tsleil-Waututh, and Musqueam nations.

Artwork on display at Historic Joy Kogawa House includes ceramics by Kate Metten, fabric applique by Judith Panson and the Japanese craft group Nuno Ehon in Sue-town near Fukuoka, and paintings by Tamiko Young.

welcome mat in the sun
Joy Kogawa House whispers
stories that light can reveal

morning shimmers
dust floats above
the snowy bed

the rocking chair
stilled
strains of lullabies

rhododendron petals
on the sidewalk
paw prints vanish

eyelet lace curtains
frame the garden
small girl sleeps

children stand
with mother
sunflowers opening

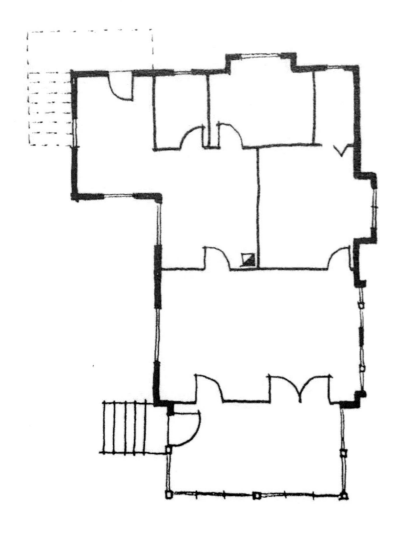

ghosts of rooms
with space to grow
repotted roses

1937- 1942 FLOOR PLAN

the cherry blossoms
wait for awe
surprised mouths agape

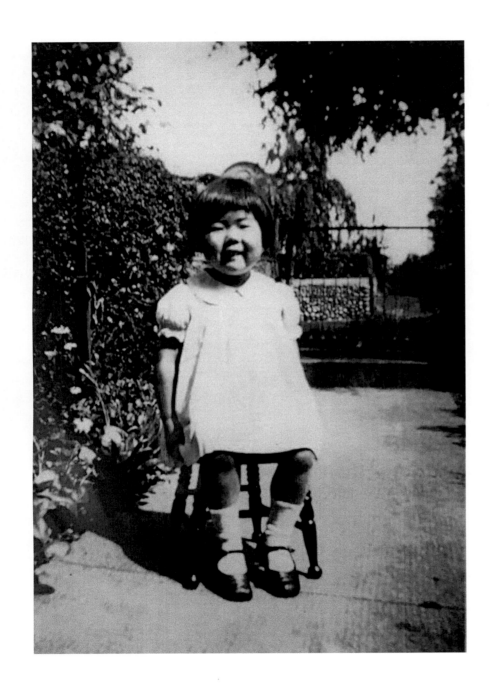

girl smiles
reminder of softer days
secret joy

nisei children
balance bowls of rice
chopsticks chirp

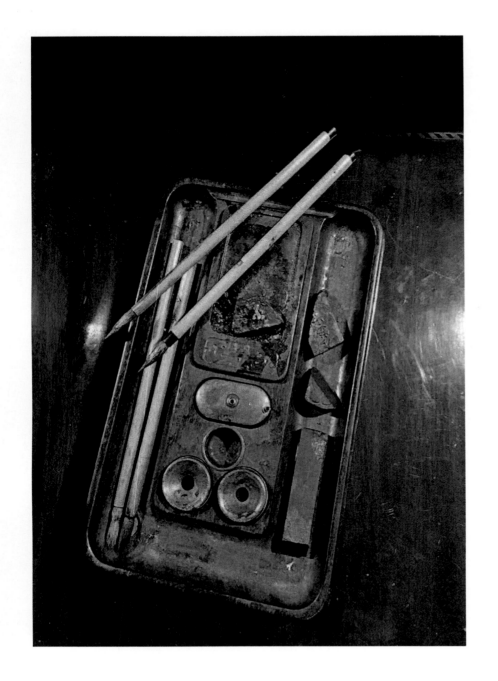

calligraphy brush
hidden in the carved case
your hand a dove

plump cherries
in a hollow bowl
small fingers choosing

a screen
painted with strokes of pastel
unfolds unity

27

steel bedstead holds heads
on hard pillows
the sound of breathing

the wainscoting draws walls
ceilings and windows
strong wooden nest

her head beneath petals
in shadowed dawn
quiet grace

piano notes drift
across the room
filtered summer light

creamy runner binds
the table
evening cool

brass shaving kit
he scrapes his face
smooth as paper

silhouette of you
in rigid cardboard
unblinking

nineteen forty-two fear
spreads sticky tar
faces break

tapestry of petals
mingle on the felt
reflection of each other

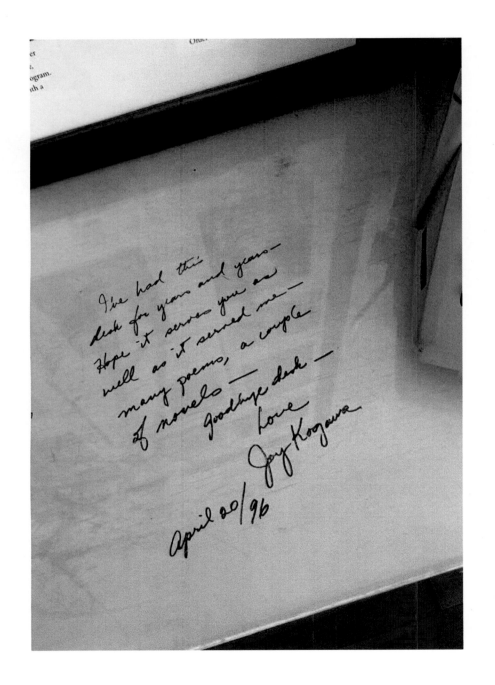

I've had this
desk for years and years—
Hope it serves you as
well as it served me—
many poems, a couple
of novels—
goodbye desk—
Love
Joy Kogawa

April 00/96

words strung together
goodbye desk
small and neat

green-keyed typewriter
wrote of loss betrayal
cold autumn breeze

summer heat
a purple fan
lifts her hair

you pick out bones
from iridescent salmon
oil drips

swoops of laughter
pour over quiet voices
bell song fills corners

love hangs in windows
on the street
a child points

suitcases wait
packed for a lifetime
time passes

clock chimes nine
a hand marked by violets
pulls the lace tight

AN APOLOGY

Apology issued by the
Anglican Bishop of Calgary and the Anglican Bishop of New Westminster
to all members of the
Japanese Canadian Community
affected by abuse perpetrated by the Reverend Canon Gordon Goichi Nakayama
(hereafter referred to as Mr. Nakayama)

1. Mr. Nakayama was a priest of the Anglican Diocese of Calgary. Some of his ministry was in the Anglican Diocese of New Westminster, and he travelled widely in Canada and in other parts of the world.
2. After he had retired, Mr. Nakayama confessed in person and in a letter dated December 28th 1994 to the then Archbishop of Calgary that he had engaged in 'sexual bad behavior . . . to so many people'.
3. Upon receipt of Mr. Nakayama's confession, the then Archbishop of Calgary formally brought forward the very serious charge of Immorality against Mr. Nakayama on February 10, 1995.
4. Upon receiving this charge, Mr. Nakayama voluntarily resigned on February 13, 1995 from the exercise of priestly ministry.
5. It is not known how many young people were affected, and no complaints were received at that time.
6. We have been made aware of the impact and effect of these past actions by some of today's survivors, whom we acknowledge and seek to support, along with those who have died, their families and friends.
7. We deeply regret that Mr. Nakayama while a priest committed these acts of immoral sexual behavior.
8. On behalf of our dioceses, we express our deep sorrow and grief for harm which Mr. Nakayama did, and we apologize to all whose lives have been affected by Mr. Nakayama's actions.
9. We deeply regret this Apology was not delivered to the Japanese Canadian Community at the time of Mr. Nakayama's confession, the charge of immorality, and his subsequent resignation from the exercise of priestly ministry.
10. We express our support to survivors, affected families, and community as a whole and deeply hope that this Apology encourages healing and wellness for all whose lives have been affected by Mr. Nakayama's actions.
11. We commit to participation in a healing and reconciliation process with the members of the Japanese Canadian Community who were harmed by Mr. Nakayama.
12. And we assure you that the Anglican Church takes these matters seriously, and takes steps to prevent this type of behaviour.

Dated at Vancouver B.C, Monday, 15 June 2015

The Right Reverend Melissa M. Skelton
Diocese of New Westminster

The Right Reverend Greg Kerr-Wilson
Diocese of Calgary

the official apology
can't lift the black stain
knees squeezed

war bonds exclude
legitimate citizens
spent ash

displacement
ink marks her fingers
as she writes

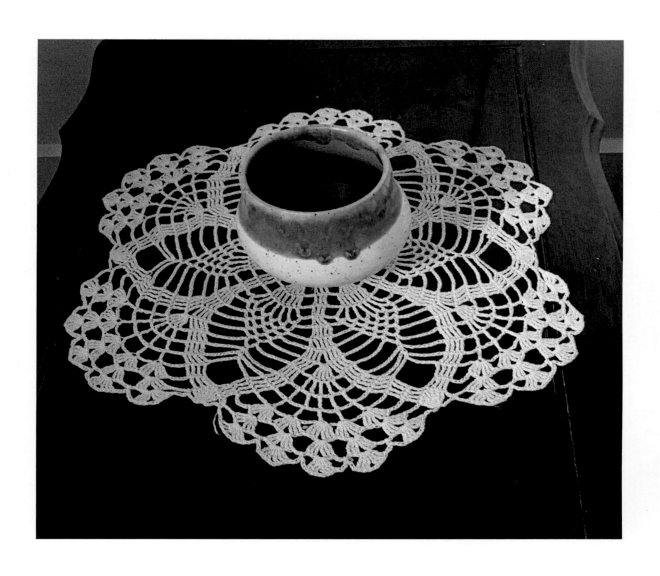

lace doily drapes
beauty onto the table
youth pales

yellowed chopsticks
lift a grain of rice
small victories

the empty tin of sesame
                crackers
        stands alone

a porcelain teapot
steams jasmine
clink of china

books on shelves
bible stories and myth
she drinks them all

the pestle grinds seeds
into fine russet powder
dust of lilies settles

trains pull them away
from grief
collective Canadian yawn

writers reflect
at Kogawa House
bread rising

a loud patriotism
waves on streets
never silent

beside the fence
mother waters roses
a bent reed

in nineteen thirty-seven
grace swells
quiet dignity

afternoon silence
pots filled with dusty webs
ache for cool water

a house in the garden
with iron pounded beams
turn back the clock

the cherry tree shivers
in the cool breeze
I wear all I own

in sunlight small windows
ablaze
glimmering eyes

stucco skin peels
walls expose spiders
breaking hurts

delicate paper
part of a whole
gasp of colour

hot oil sighs
after lunch
family matters

eyes the hue of mud
glance at the camera
river ice melting

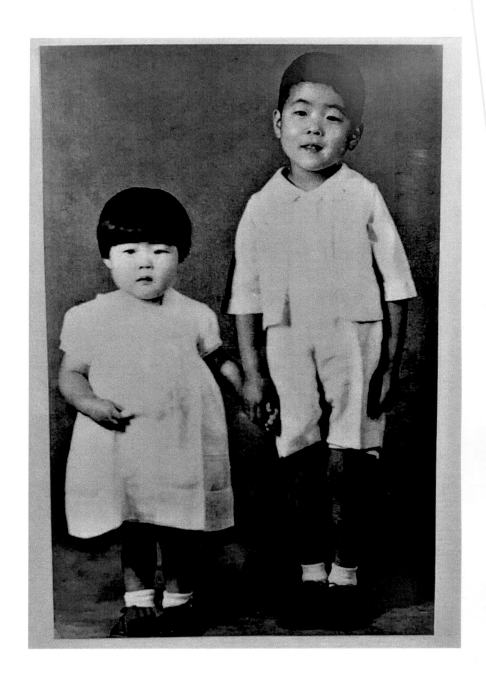

write out your pain
blind injustice festers
remember

light caresses the bed
where you sleep
harvest moon

cupped by wind
she flies overhead
floating

check the mirror
treacle skin black hair
injustice bleeds

rows of children
captured in a photo
stilled butterflies

water pitcher
remembers silver
sprinkle of rain

state of mind
a writer's soft bed
castles of clay

About the Author

Jude Neale is a Canadian poet, vocalist, spoken word performer, and mentor. She publishes frequently in journals, anthologies, and e-zines, and has been short-listed, highly commended, and a finalist in many international competitions. Jude has written eight books, to date. Her book, *A Quiet Coming of Light, A Poetic Memoir* (Leaf Press) was a finalist for the Pat Lowther Memorial Award, in recognition of Canadian female poets.

One of Jude's poems from her book, *Splendid in Its Silence*, was chosen by Britain's Poet Laureate to ride with other winners around the Channel Islands on public transit for a year, and she was a featured reader at the Guernsey International Literary Festival. This book was an SPM Prize winner and was published in the UK. Some of the poems in this collection can be heard on Jude's collaborative (viola/spoken word) EP, *Places Beyond* with the renowned composer and viola player, Thomas Beckman. Jude and Thomas subsequently performed the world premiere of their original *St. Roch Suite* with the Prince George Symphony Orchestra.

Jude and Bonnie Nish started an online collaboration in 2018 which led them to write *Cantata in Two Voices* (Ekstasis Editions) in fifty challenging days. She had two books, *A Blooming* (Ekstasis Editions) and *We Sing Ourselves Back*, published in 2019.

Her eighth book, *Impromptu,* was launched in 2020, and that year Jude was a writer-in-residence at Historic Joy Kogawa House, where she wrote her book, *Inside the Pearl*. Jude published *The River Answers* (Ekstasis Editions), in 2021.

About the Photographer

Paul Hooson is a professional stage, street, and therapeutic clown, former student of Marcel Marceau and Etienne Decroux, and was a member of the influential *"Palais des Merveilles"* street theatre company in Paris in 1971/1972.

Paul created silent clown "Alexander" in 1975, cofounded ground-breaking bilingual clown theatre company *"Cirque Alexander"* with Anita Couvrette (Officer O'Sneeley) in 1977, and formed the *"Mirth Unit" Therapeutic Clown Program* at B.C. Children's Hospital in 1994, becoming Canada's first Therapeutic Clown Doctor.

Paul is also a professional puppeteer, and has an extensive resumé in film and television, including *Stargate SG1/Atlantis*, *The Santa Claus 2*, *Scary Movie 3*, *Alien vs. Predator Requiem*, and *i, Robot*. He was honoured to be key puppeteer and artistic collaborator for Fred Penner's stage show *"The Cat Came Back,"* which toured nationally in 2012 and 2013.